Please renew/return this item by the last date shown.
Please call the number below:

Renewals and enquiries: 0300 123 4049

Textphone for hearing or
speech impaired users: 0300 123 4041

www.hertsdirect.org/librarycatalogue

Hertfordshire

L32

STEP-UP
HISTORY

Anglo-Saxon Invaders and Settlers

Peter D. Riley

Evans

Published by Evans Brothers Limited
2A Portman Mansions
Chiltern Street
London W1U 6NR

Reprinted 2008

© Evans Brothers Limited 2006

Produced for Evans Brothers Limited by
White-Thomson Publishing Ltd,
Bridgewater Business Centre,
210 High Street,
Lewes, East Sussex BN7 2NH

Printed in Hong Kong by New Era Printing Co. Ltd.

Project manager: Ruth Nason

Designer: Helen Nelson, Jet the Dog

Consultant: Rosie Turner-Bisset, Reader in
Education and Director of Learning and
Teaching, Faculty of Education, University of
Middlesex.

British Library Cataloguing in Publication Data

Riley, Peter D.

   Anglo-Saxon invaders and settlers - (Step-up
   history)
   1. Anglo-Saxons - Great Britain - Juvenile
   literature
   2. Great Britain - History - Anglo-Saxon period,
   449-1066 - Juvenile literature
   I. Title
   942'.014

ISBN: 978 0 237 53038 9

Picture acknowledgements:

The Bridgeman Art Library: page 22t (British
Library, London, UK/www.bridgeman.co.uk); The
Trustees of the British Museum: pages 14b, 16t,
16b, 26l; Canterbury Archaeological Trust: cover
(top right) and pages 6l, 6r, 20, 21c, 25l; Corbis:
pages 4 (Hulton-Deutsch Collection), 9 (Archivo
Iconografico S. A.), 26r (Bettmann); Exile Images:
page 5t; Historic Scotland Photographic Library:
page 11 (Crown Copyright reproduced courtesy of
Historic Scotland); Michael Nason: pages 12t, 12b,
21b; the National Trust, Sutton Hoo: page 15;
Topfoto.co.uk: cover (top left) and pages 5b
(Museum of London), 7 (HIP/The British Museum),
10 (The British Library), 13 (PAL), 14t (HIP/The
British Museum), 14c (HIP/The British Museum), 17
(HIP), 18, 25r (The British Museum); West Stow
Anglo-Saxon Village: cover (main) and pages 1,
21t, 22b, 23, 24.

Maps and diagrams by Helen Nelson.

Contents

People on the move

Many people today move from one part of Britain to another. Some move to find a better job. Some students move away to college when they are about 18 years old. After college they may settle in another part of the country or even in a different country. When people move from one country to live in another, they are said to emigrate. When they enter another country to settle in it they are called immigrants.

Find out about your family

If you ask older members of your family about where your family came from, you may find that your family came from another part of the country. For example, many people living in industrial towns in Britain have families that once lived in the countryside. They moved into the towns to find work in the nineteenth century. You may find that some members of your family have emigrated to another country such as Australia, Canada or the United States.

◀ *The people on this ship were leaving Britain, nearly 100 years ago, to settle in Australia. Were they immigrants or emigrants?*

These people moved away from their homes in Sudan because of war and famine.

In the news

On the television news you may see reports about people leaving one country to become immigrants in another. Often these people move not just to find a better job but to try to find any kind of work, as there are too few jobs in their own country.

In some countries where there is civil war people are attacked because of their religion or the ethnic group to which they belong. These people may move away to find safety. For many people moving home is upsetting, but what must it be like if you have to move because your life is threatened?

Invaders and settlers

In this book we will find out about some 'people on the move' from hundreds of years ago. The Anglo-Saxons first came to Britain as invaders and many battles took place. Eventually the invaders settled in England and more of their people entered peacefully as immigrants. They are the ancestors of many people in the country today.

▼ *The Anglo-Saxon invaders used spears like these.*

Who were the Anglo-Saxons?

In the fifth century there were people living in Europe called Angles, Saxons and Jutes. They became known as Anglo-Saxons when they moved across to England.

In their homelands these people were farmers and traders, but they also formed armies to defend themselves.

Evidence from grave goods

Some of the people buried their dead in graves. They buried items with the body, which they thought would help the dead person in the afterlife. A wide range of these items, known as grave goods, have been found and they have helped archaeologists to find out about the people's way of life.

The grave goods included cups and horns containing drink, dishes for holding food, and even food such as a joint of meat, duck eggs and oysters. There were also possessions of the dead person. A man was buried with his sword, spear and shield. A woman was buried with needles and combs. Both men and women were buried with their jewellery.

▶ *This pendant made from gold and garnets was found in an Anglo-Saxon grave in Canterbury.*

◀ *This skeleton of a woman buried with grave goods was found at Buckland Anglo-Saxon cemetery, near Dover.*

Clues from cremation pots

Other Anglo-Saxon people cremated their dead and put the ashes in cremation pots. The pots were then buried. Pieces of land were set aside for the burial of cremation pots and they became cemeteries. Some cemeteries contain over a thousand pots.

▶ *This cremation pot dates from the fifth or sixth century – about 1500 years ago.*

How long ago?

You can get a sense of how long ago the Anglo-Saxons came to England by making a row of 31 people. Each person represents a lifetime of 50 years. The first in line was born 50 years ago, the second was born 100 years ago … and the thirty-first person was born just after the Anglo-Saxons arrived in England. They might have been one of the first Anglo-Saxon immigrants born in England.

Grave goods were not usually buried with the cremation pots. However, the pots themselves tell us about the skill of the Anglo-Saxon potters. The pots had different styles. Some were bowl-shaped while others were shaped like a vase. Most had designs on them and some designs were quite complicated.

| 50 years ago | 100 years ago | 150 years ago | 200 years ago | 250 years ago | 300 years ago | 350 years ago | 400 years ago | 450 years |

The end of Roman Britain

In AD 43, long before the Anglo-Saxons, the Romans invaded Britain. Britain became a province of the Roman Empire. At this time Britain was inhabited by people called Celts.

As the Romans conquered the country they built roads and towns. People from other parts of the Empire travelled along the roads to trade in the towns, and a pottery industry was set up in Britain for trade with other provinces. Life was well organised and many of the Celts changed to the Roman way of life.

The red lines show roads built by the Romans. The town names are modern.

Antonine Wall
Hadrian's Wall
Carlisle
South Shields
York
Chester
Lincoln
Wroxeter
Leicester
Caistor
Droitwich
Cambridge
Kentchester
Colchester
Gloucester
Caerwent
St Albans
Cirencester
London
Bath
Silchester
Canterbury
Winchester
Dorchester
Chichester
Exeter

Your local Roman road

You may or may not live in a settlement that was first set up by the Anglo-Saxons (see page 19), but you may live close to a road that served the Roman Empire. Compare this map of the main Roman roads with a map of Britain in an atlas. Locate where you live on the Roman road map. Which Roman road is the nearest to where you live?

Soldiers in the Roman army

The Romans had part of their army stationed in Britain to defend the province and to prevent rebellions. Not all the soldiers in the army were Romans. Some were hired fighters called mercenaries who came from countries in the Empire or from outside it. The Anglo-Saxon homelands were outside the Empire but some men from there joined the Roman army. We know this because Roman army uniforms have been found as grave goods buried in the Anglo-Saxon homelands.

Roman soldiers in a ship. Some Anglo-Saxons were hired fighters in the Roman army.

The army leaves Britain

By the end of the fourth century many boundaries of the Roman Empire were under attack. Gradually legions of the Roman army in Britain were called away to help defend the rest of the Empire. By 410 the whole army had gone and the British were left to defend themselves.

Without the Romans, life in Britain became disorganised. Archaeologists have found evidence that pottery production stopped. This suggests that trade stopped too.

The British ask for help

The British were unable to organise a strong army and there were frequent attacks at this time, from north of the Antonine Wall, by people called the Picts. The British elected a leader called Vortigern. He knew that the Anglo-Saxons were good warriors because some had been in the Roman army in Britain. Vortigern asked the Anglo-Saxons for help. Two brothers called Hengest and Horsa arrived with three ships full of warriors.

The Anglo-Saxons arrive

The Anglo-Saxon Chronicles are written accounts of events in England from year 1 (the year of the birth of Christ) until year 1154. The early parts of the Chronicles were written by monks in the ninth century. For information about events that happened before then, the monks used the work of earlier writers, such as Bede (see page 18). Later on, descriptions of events were written down at the time that they happened.

The Anglo-Saxon Chronicles show that the Anglo-Saxons arrived in Britain to help Vortigern, the leader of the British, in 449.

From the part of the account shown here, what did Vortigern give the Anglo-Saxons (the Angles) in return for them defending England from the Picts? Were they successful in fighting the Picts? What messages did they send back to Angel, their home country?

▶ *This extract from the year 449 of the Anglo-Saxon Chronicles says that the Angles landed at Ebbesfleet. This is near Sandwich in Kent. In the circle at the top you can see some writing from the original documents of the Chronicles.*

....In their days the Angles were invited here by King Vortigern and they came to Britain in three longships, landing at Ebbesfleet. King Vortigern gave them territory in the south east of this land, on condition that they fight the Picts. This they did and had victory wherever they went. They then sent to Angel, commanded more aid, and commanded that they should be told of the Britons' worthlessness and the choice nature of the land. They soon sent hither a greater host to help the others ... Their war-leaders were Hengest and Horsa, who were Wihtgil's sons. First of all, they killed and drove away the king's enemies; then later they turned on the king and the British, destroying through fire and the sword's edge.

Information sent home to Angel

It is thought that the word 'worthlessness' (in line 13 of the extract on page 10) refers to the Britons' weakness – so the Angles were suggesting that the British would be easy to fight. What words would we use today? The 'choice nature' of the land means that it is good farmland. These two pieces of information would encourage more people from Angel to come to Britain.

Attacks on the British

According to the Chronicles, the Anglo-Saxons began attacking the British in the year they arrived (449) and the attacks continued. In 455 the army of Hengest and Horsa fought Vortigern's army and won. Horsa was killed in the battle. Eighteen years later Hengest was still fighting the British. What year was this?

King Arthur

The last leader of the British to fight the Anglo-Saxons was called Arthur. He won a battle in 495 which started the legend of 'King Arthur'. In 515 he was killed in another battle with the Anglo-Saxons. Use http://www.battle1066.com/arthur.shtml to find out how the legend of King Arthur began. Make a list of the people who helped to develop it.

◄ Many Pictish stones have been found in Scotland. The carvings on this one show three scenes from a battle between Picts (on the left) and Angles (right). Which side is winning? The Picts raided the north of England until 711, when they were completely defeated.

Sutton Hoo

There are fifteen mounds of earth called barrows on a hillside at Sutton Hoo in Suffolk. In the top of some of the barrows there are hollows. They indicate that in the past people have dug into them to find out what was inside.

In 1938 Mrs Edith Pretty, the owner of the land on which the barrows were built, hired an archaeologist to find out what they contained.

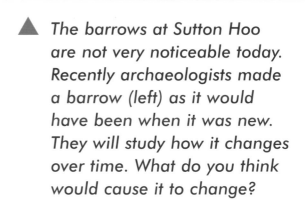

▲ The barrows at Sutton Hoo are not very noticeable today. Recently archaeologists made a barrow (left) as it would have been when it was new. They will study how it changes over time. What do you think would cause it to change?

How large?

The largest barrow was 30 metres long, 4.5 metres wide and 3 metres high. Measure out these dimensions of the barrow in the school hall or yard to realise how large it is.

The first finds

The archaeologist, Basil Brown, dug into three barrows and found that two contained cremations. The third had had a boat buried in it. All three barrows had been dug open before and had been robbed. The only remains of the boat were a few rusty nails. However, the robbers had left behind some fragments of pottery. These were identified as Anglo-Saxon, made in the sixth and seventh centuries.

The largest barrow

In 1939 Mr Brown began digging into another barrow. It was the largest barrow on the site. After a few days he found rows of rusty nails arranged as if in the side of a ship. The contents of this barrow had not been raided and so he could carefully remove the soil to reveal the ship's hull. The wooden parts of the ship had rotted away but had stained the sand around it. By exposing the rows of nails and stained sand, Mr Brown discovered the shape and size of the ship.

When Mr Brown began moving soil from the centre of the ship, he discovered two iron rings. He used a soft brush to remove the sand and found some corroded bronze material. A team of archaeologists was called in to begin removing these items. As they did so, they found that a wooden hut had been built in the centre of the ship. Inside they discovered the largest amount of buried treasure ever found in Britain.

▲ *The soil had to be removed very carefully so as not to disturb the nails.*

▼ *Robbers had dug into the top of the largest barrow but they had not disturbed the place where the ship was buried. They had not found the hut full of treasure in the centre of the ship.*

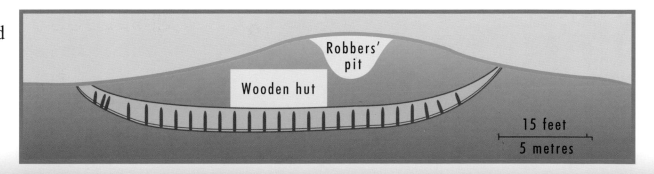

Robbers'
pit

Wooden hut

15 feet
5 metres

Why was the ship buried?

Archaeologists sometimes find buried ships. The ships have sunk and been covered in sand or silt. Some Viking ships have been found buried in this way and one Anglo-Saxon ship was found buried in a peat bog. The Sutton Hoo ship was different. It had been pulled up a hill and buried. This suggests that the ship was special. The presence of treasure in the ship suggests that it was very special.

Before removing the treasures, archaeologists made notes of the positions in which they were found. Here are some of the treasures.

▲ *The style and decoration of these gold coins tell archaeologists that they were probably made about 620. Archaeologists think that the coins and other treasures were buried shortly after then.*

◀ *This object decorated with gold and garnets was the lid of a leather purse that was worn around the waist.*

▼ *The sword was kept inside a wooden scabbard lined with sheep's wool. The handle is richly decorated. The blade is 84cm long.*

Was someone buried there?

Once it was thought that the buried ship at Sutton Hoo was a monument to an important person. No skeleton or bones had been found. If they had been, this would have shown that the barrow was possibly a burial place.

After the treasures had been removed, the ship was buried again. Then, in 1966, archaeologists uncovered it once more in order to make plaster casts of the ship's hull. They also decided to test the soil under the ship for signs of phosphate. Skeletons contain large amounts of this chemical so, if a skeleton had rotted away completely, more phosphate would be found in the soil than normal.

The soil under the ship was found to contain more phosphate than normal, but spread about so the position of the skeleton could not be worked out. However, the iron of the sword found in the barrow was also tested and found to have more phosphate than normal. This suggested that the sword had been lying next to a large source of phosphate – a skeleton.

This fitted in with observations made of grave goods in other Anglo-Saxon burials, where a sword was buried next to the body. The position of the skeleton at Sutton Hoo was found to be in the middle of the treasure. The barrow was the grave of a wealthy pagan, who had been buried surrounded by possessions.

▼ *At Sutton Hoo today you can see this reconstruction of the burial.*

Grave goods

If people were buried with grave goods today, what items do you think would be buried with a rich and important person?

15

A look at the treasures

What would it be like to find buried treasure? Imagine sweeping soil away with a soft brush and seeing a piece of gold glinting out at you. When the archaeologists began excavating at the centre of the Sutton Hoo ship, they must have been excited as they carefully removed the soil and lifted out their finds.

Gold is unusual in that it does not corrode. Other materials do change. Silver tarnishes, iron rusts, and bone, ivory and wood rot away. Some of the treasures in the Sutton Hoo burial were made partly of materials that survived through the centuries and partly of materials that rotted away. This meant that they had broken up where the perishable materials had disappeared. When these damaged treasures were removed they were cleaned and new materials were added to them in order to restore them.

▲ Most of the shield was made of wood which rotted away. This shield is a reconstruction using the original metal pieces of the shield with new pieces of wood. Its diameter is almost 84cm.

◀ More silver was found at Sutton Hoo than in any other grave. These bowls (22.5cm diameter) were part of a set of ten. The bowls and the spoons, which are 25cm long, were made in Greece.

The helmet

One of the most important finds from the Sutton Hoo ship is the helmet. This had broken into about 500 fragments but archaeologists studied them and put them back together like the pieces in a jigsaw puzzle so that we can see how the helmet originally looked. Much of the helmet is made of iron, but the parts covering the centre of the face are made of bronze.

Skilful designs

The treasures have many skilfully made designs on them. One design feature that is found on many of the treasures is the shape of a bird. If you look carefully at the front of the helmet you can see the wings of a bird forming the eyebrows. The head can be seen in the centre of the forehead. The body covers the nose and the tail covers the upper lip like a moustache! The shield also carries a design of a bird of prey.

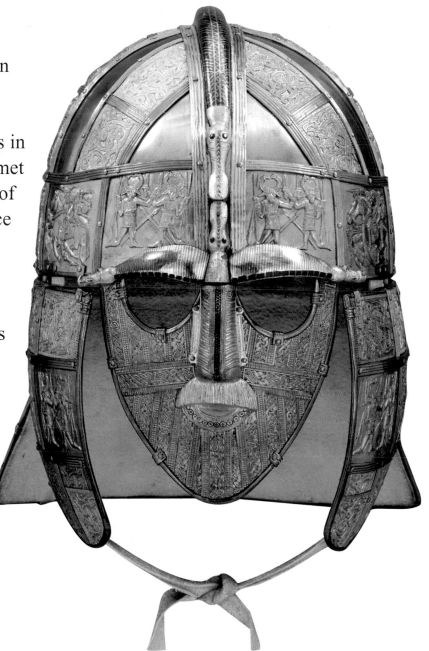

It is thought that the helmet was a *ceremonial* object like a crown. It does not have any dents in it that could have been made by a sword and this suggests that it was never worn as armour in battle.

A bird symbol

Birds used to represent strength and courage. Select a bird from a bird book that you think represents these sentiments and draw it into a design for a shield.

Where the Anglo-Saxons came from

Historians use written evidence to help them find out about the past. One of the most important writers in Anglo-Saxon times was a monk called Bede (673-735), who lived at Jarrow Abbey in Northumberland.

Bede gives a description of where the Anglo-Saxons came from and where they settled in England. The names Bede uses for the places where the Anglo-Saxons came from were also used at later times. This has made it easy for historians to find them.

They came from three of the stronger peoples of Germany, the Saxons, the Angles and the Jutes. From the Jutes came the Cantuarii [the people of Kent] and the Victuarii who are the people who occupy the Isle of Wight and those who live opposite the Isle of Wight, on the mainland, in the territory of the West Saxons and are to this day called the nation of Jutes. From the Saxons, that is the region that is now called Old Saxony, came the East Saxons, the South Saxons and the West Saxons. From the Angles, that is the country which is called Angeln and which from then till now has remained deserted, and which lies between the lands of the Saxons and the Jutes, came the east Angles, the Middle Angles, the Mercians, and all of the Northumbrian race, that is the people who live north of the Humber as well as the other Anglian tribes.

▲ From this information provided by Bede it has been possible to make a map showing the paths the Anglo-Saxons took as they emigrated to England.

Archaeologists have confirmed the information provided by Bede by studying cremation pots. They have found that pottery made in the homelands of the Jutes is also found in Kent. Pottery from Saxony is also found in Cambridgeshire (East Saxons) and pottery found in Angeln is also found in Nottinghamshire (Middle Angles).

Place names

Anglo-Saxons gave names to the places where they settled. The names described a feature of the place. For example, they ended with:

- –bury (fortified place)
- –caster or –chester (town)
- –ford (river crossing)
- –ley or –leigh (forest)
- –shaw (small wood)
- –stoke or –stock (religious place)
- –wick (farm).

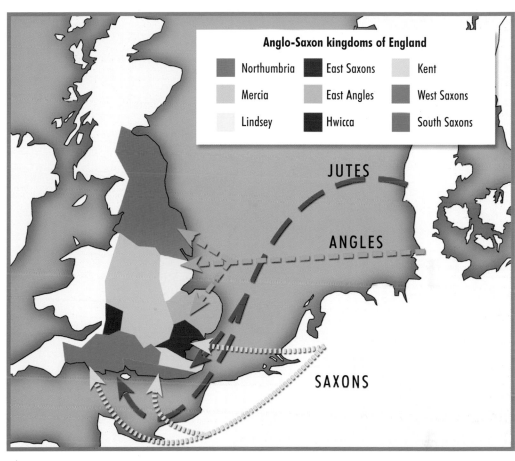

Anglo-Saxon kingdoms of England

- Northumbria
- Mercia
- Lindsey
- East Saxons
- East Angles
- Hwicca
- Kent
- West Saxons
- South Saxons

JUTES

ANGLES

SAXONS

▲ *This map shows the homelands of the Anglo-Saxons and the journeys they made to reach and settle in England.*

BIRMINGHAM

▶ *Birmingham is made from three Anglo-Saxon words: Beornmund (the name of a tribe leader), ing (a group of people) and ham (estate). Together they meant the estate of Beornmund's people.*

On the map

Find a modern map of England and look at a part of the country where the Anglo-Saxons settled. What Anglo-Saxon place names can you find?

Anglo-Saxon settlements

Many towns and villages date back to Anglo-Saxon times. This means that there must be the remains of Anglo-Saxon homes under some of the houses and shops that we see today. The problem is that archaeologists cannot reach them.

In a few places archaeologists have found the remains of villages that have not been built over. These settlements can sometimes be discovered by looking from an aeroplane at patterns of mounds in the landscape.

Excavating these abandoned villages gives archaeologists many clues as to how the Anglo-Saxons lived.

Houses

Anglo-Saxons used building materials such as wood and reeds, which rot easily and leave no trace. However, post-holes remain in the ground, and these show the outline of the floor of a house.

▼ *You can see the post-holes in this view from above of an Anglo-Saxon house that was excavated in Kent.*

Plan of a house

Mark out a 10cm x 6cm rectangle on paper in black circles about 0.5cm in diameter, using the photograph of post-holes to help you. You have made a model of the outline of an Anglo-Saxon house.

The wooden posts that were placed in the post-holes formed part of a framework to which plank walls and reed thatched roofs were attached.

Reconstructions

Archaeologists have used information collected from the ground to reconstruct Anglo-Saxon houses. At West Stow in Suffolk an Anglo-Saxon village has been built, and people re-enact what life was like there in those times.

The farmer's house at West Stow Anglo-Saxon Village was made of oak and thatch. The people are dressed in early Anglo-Saxon costume.

◀ *This drawing shows the framework to which walls and roof were fixed.*

Churches

Monks travelled through England converting many Anglo-Saxons to Christianity and stone churches were built for worship. Many of these churches have been modified over the years and so the Anglo-Saxon features may have been removed. Find out about the history of your local parish church. Are any parts of it Anglo-Saxon?

◀ *If you visit a church today, you may find some parts of it that were part of the original Anglo-Saxon building. This archway in a church in Warwickshire is from Anglo-Saxon times. The stained-glass window was made in the twentieth century.*

Anglo-Saxon farmers

Most Anglo-Saxons were farmers. Farming families lived together in small villages and farmed the land around them.

The farming year

The year began with ploughing to break up the soil so that seeds could be sown. Wheat, oats and barley were sown and these crops were left to grow until late summer. By then the tops of the plant stalks were heavy with swollen cereal grains. The men harvested the crops by cutting them down with scythes and threshing the stalks to separate them from the grains.

▲ Oxen were used to pull the plough but a man was needed to steer the plough and this was hard work.

Sheep were reared for wool and meat. In spring the ewes and lambs had to be cared for so that the size of the flock would increase. In summer the sheep were shorn and just before winter many were slaughtered and their meat cut up for later use.

Cattle were reared for their milk, meat and hides. Pigs were reared simply for their meat. Evidence for the animals eaten in a village comes from the bones that were thrown away outside the houses after meals.

◄ Farm animals were smaller in Anglo-Saxon times than they are now. These Norfolk horned sheep at West Stow Anglo-Saxon Village are smaller than the sheep you see in fields today.

From pictures, carvings and poetry there is evidence that some farm work was carried out mainly by men and some mainly by women. The women's work linked with that of the men. After threshing, women used stones called querns to grind the cereal grains into flour for bread and cakes.

Women milked the cattle and made some of the milk into butter and cheese. They preserved the meat by hanging it over a smoky fire or by rubbing salt into it. These processes stopped the meat going bad and kept it edible through the winter. When the sheep were shorn, women spun the wool into yarn and wove this into cloth.

▲ *In this house at the West Stow Anglo-Saxon Village the woman on the left is spinning wool, using a drop spindle.*

Bartering

Anglo-Saxons did have money, but some trade was done by bartering. For example, a farmer wanting to buy another's cow would offer a few sheep for it. The farmer with the cow might ask for more or perhaps for a few chickens. Eventually the farmers agreed a deal. Draw and cut out a set of farm animals and crops and try trading them, by bartering, with those of a friend.

Around the home

There were other tasks around the home. Chickens and ducks had to be fed and their eggs collected. Vegetables such as carrots, onions and cabbages were grown in plots of land close to the home. Bees were reared in hives and the honey collected was used for food or for making mead. Herbs were grown close to the home or collected from the countryside to make medicines to treat ailments in the family.

Anglo-Saxon crafts

Some people in the village farmed the land for part of the time but worked at a craft at other times. This helped to provide the villagers with the items they needed for survival.

The potter

Pottery was used to provide containers for food – particularly bowls. The potter would dig out the clay, mix it with water, remove stones and then mix in sand, crushed shells or even grass to help the clay bind together.

In early Anglo-Saxon times the potter would make a bowl from strips of clay shaped like long sausages. These were coiled around to make the base and sides of the bowl.

After AD 900, potters used a wheel. A lump of clay was placed in the middle of the wheel and spun while the potter shaped the clay with an animal rib bone or piece of wood.

Make an Anglo-Saxon bowl

Roll out lumps of Plasticine to make long thin sausages. Coil one to make the bowl base, then coil another around the edge to start the wall of the pot. Coil more Plasticine sausages one on top of another to make the bowl wall. Then smooth the sides to fill the gaps between the coils.

After the bowls had been shaped they were left to dry, then heated strongly in a kiln to make the clay hard and rigid.

◀ *Pots, loom weights (doughnut shaped), dice and beads are some of the pottery items made by these men re-enacting life at West Stow Anglo-Saxon Village.*

The carpenter

The carpenter knew which woods in the forest had the best properties for making particular objects. Items made by the carpenter ranged from handles for farmers' forks and spades to cups, plates, furniture and storage chests. The carpenter also cut and shaped planks for making barrels, buckets and butter churns.

The bone and antler worker

Bones from farm animals were used to make spoons, needles, pins and buckles. Hollow bones were used to make whistles and pipes for playing music. Antler is tougher than bone and was used to make combs. Some people have said that Anglo-Saxons used bone and antlers as we use plastics today.

▼ *This Anglo-Saxon comb was carved from antler.*

The glassworker

Glass was made from a mixture of sand, potash and natron. This was heated in an oven for a few days, during which the glassworker regularly stirred it to release bubbles of gas. The glass that formed as the mixture cooled had a green tinge, but coloured glass could be made by adding minerals containing copper.

The molten glass was shaped using metal tools to make beads for jewellery and beakers for drinking.

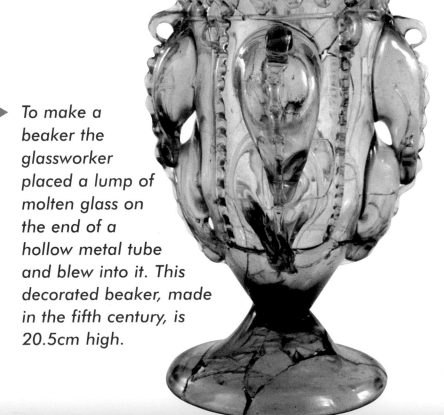

▶ *To make a beaker the glassworker placed a lump of molten glass on the end of a hollow metal tube and blew into it. This decorated beaker, made in the fifth century, is 20.5cm high.*

So who was buried in the ship?

When archaeologists discover a site they try to find out as much as possible about it. They also review their finds as they go along, to help them understand what they have found.

If we review what we have seen about the Sutton Hoo ship, we know that it was built for somebody very special – perhaps a leader. The helmet and shield suggest that the person buried there was a man. There is also evidence that the man was wealthy – perhaps the leader of a kingdom. He could in fact be a king.

Symbols of authority

We have seen that the helmet could have been used as a sign of office like a crown. There was also another item that could have been used in this way. It is a whetstone – a stone used to sharpen swords.

The whetstone found in the ship burial is larger than usual and has smooth sides, which indicate that it has never been used. It is also highly decorated. For all these reasons it is thought that the whetstone was a symbol of authority. The symbol suggested that the owner held the means by which his soldiers could sharpen their swords.

◀ The top of the whetstone is decorated with a brass stag.

▲ Elizabeth II was crowned queen in 1953. At the coronation ceremony an orb and sceptre were used as symbols of office of the British monarchy. It is thought that the Sutton Hoo whetstone was used as a symbol in a similar way.

The funeral of a king

Historians have found that part of an Anglo-Saxon poem called 'Beowulf' describes the funeral of Scyld, a Danish king. What differences and similarities do you notice between the description in the poem (right) and the burial at Sutton Hoo?

King Raedwald

In his History, Bede wrote about King Raedwald, who died and was buried about 625. This was the same time as suggested for the Sutton Hoo burial by the coins found there (see page 14).

Bede says that Raedwald was Christian but also kept his pagan ways. Silver items, such as spoons, are given to someone after they have been baptised and become a Christian. The two silver spoons in the Sutton Hoo treasure might suggest that the person had been baptised, while the other grave goods suggest pagan ways. From these pieces of evidence it is believed that King Raedwald was buried in the ship. But no one can be really sure.

Then Scyld departed at the destined hour,
That powerful man sought the Lord's protection,
His own close companions carried him
Down to the sea, so he, lord of the Danes,
had asked while he could speak.
That well-loved man had ruled his land for many years.
There in the harbour stood the ring prow ship,
The princes vessel, icy eager to sail;
And then they laid their dear lord,
The giver of rings, deep within the ship
By the mast in majesty; many treasures
And adornments from far and wide were gathered there.
I have never heard of a ship equipped
More handsomely with weapons and war-gear,
swords corslets; on his breast
lay countless treasures that were to travel far
with him into the waves domain.

Possessions

Can things be deduced about a person from their possessions? Collect ten things you own. Write down what you think they say about you. Give them to a friend and ask him or her to write down what they think the items say about you. Do the two sets of notes match?

Glossary

afterlife
the life that some people believe continues after a person has died.

antler
one of a pair of bony branches that grow from the head of some deer.

archaeologists
people who study history by excavating sites inhabited in the past.

baptise
to perform a religious ceremony in which a person becomes a Christian. It may involve sprinkling water on the person, or dipping them in water.

barrow
an ancient mound built from earth.

bartering
exchanging goods without using money.

butter churn
a device in which milk is shaken about to make it into butter.

cemeteries
places where people are buried. Note that when people are buried around a church, this is called the churchyard, not a cemetery.

ceremonial
used in ceremonies.

Christ
the name Christians give to Jesus, who they believe is the Son of God.

civil war
a war in which people in the same country fight each other.

convert
to change someone's beliefs.

corrode
to break up due to the action of chemicals.

cremate
to burn a dead body, so that it becomes ash.

deduce
to make conclusions.

emigrate
to leave a country to settle in another.

empire
a large area, which may comprise many countries, ruled by one people.

estate
a large area of land owned by one person or family.

ethnic group
a group of people who belong to the same nation and share the same traditions, for example in the way they dress and the food they eat.

excavate
to dig a site, for archaeological study.

famine
a time when there is little food for people to eat.

finds
items that have been discovered by archaeologists investigating a site.

fragments
pieces of a broken object.

garnets
a type of deep red stone used for decoration in jewellery.

grave goods
items put in a person's grave to help them in the afterlife.

hull
the part of a ship that is in contact with the water when the ship floats.

immigrant
a person who moves into a country in order to settle there.

invaders
people who enter a country with the intention of ruling it.

kiln
a furnace used for heating clay to make pottery.

legend
a story told for generations about someone who was imagined to have lived in the past but with no historical evidence to support it.

legion	a division of the Roman army with 3,000 to 6,000 soldiers in it.
mead	an alcoholic drink made from fermented honey and water.
mercenaries	soldiers hired by people in a foreign country to fight for them.
minerals	rocky substances rich in certain chemicals such as copper or iron.
monks	men who live under strict religious rules such as taking part in acts of worship several times each day.
monument	a structure often made of stone, put up in honour of a person or an event.
natron	a substance, also called soda, which contains the chemicals sodium, carbon and oxygen.
pagans	a general term used for people who follow a religion which is not one of the major world religions.
peat bog	a swampy area with large amounts of plant material which has not completely rotted down.
perishable	liable to break down or rot if conditions are suitable.
phosphate	a chemical containing phosphorus and oxygen which is used by the body to make bones and teeth.
plaster cast	a mould of an object made in plaster.
potash	a substance made from wood ash, containing the chemical potassium.
province	a division of an empire.
quern	a device made from specially shaped stones for grinding corn into flour.

raid	to make a rapid attack taking people by surprise.
rebellion	organised attack on the rulers of a country by people in the country who do not wish to follow the rulers' laws.
reconstruction	a drawing or model, based on evidence, representing what something may have been like.
restore	to repair something so that it appears as if it is new.
scythe	a farm implement with a long curved blade which is swung in fields of ripe crops to cut the crop stalks.
settle	to stop moving around and stay in one place.
settlement	a place where people have settled.
silt	tiny fragments of rock that are similar to sand grains.
site	a place where an archaeological investigation is made.
tarnish	to form a coating on a silver surface as the silver reacts with chemicals in the air.
territory	land that belongs to someone.
thresh	to separate grain from corn stalks by beating.
warrior	person with skills in using weapons and prepared to fight in a war.
whetstone	a stone which is moistened with water and used to sharpen metal blades.
yarn	a thread made by spinning textile fibres such as wool together.

For teachers and parents

This book is designed to support and extend the learning objectives for unit 6B of the QCA History Scheme of Work.

Three European peoples, the Angles, Saxons and Jutes, came across to England, settled and became known as the Anglo-Saxons. They arrived after the Romans left Britain and gradually spread out through most of England. They built wooden houses, which have rotted away, but towards the end of Anglo-Saxon times they built churches in stone and a few survive to this day. Most of the others have been extended and rebuilt at various times in history and their Saxon origins have disappeared or can only be seen in the remains of a wall or a window.

The Saxons left few buildings but many artefacts. The pagan Anglo-Saxons buried their dead with grave goods – items from the person's life thought to help them in the afterlife. These items have helped archaeologists build up a picture of Anglo-Saxon daily life. At the start of the Anglo-Saxon period there were few written documents, but by the end of the period laws had been written down which are of great value to historians in understanding how the people lived.

In early Anglo-Saxon times there were many leaders of Anglo-Saxon groups who called themselves kings, but eventually one king emerged who ruled all the land – King Alfred of Wessex. Much of his time was spent dealing with the Vikings, who had settled in Northern and Eastern England, and gradually pushing them out of the country. The last Anglo-Saxon king, Harold, defeated the last Viking to try to claim the English crown in 1066. Later that year Harold died at the Battle of Hastings. The Anglo-Saxon period came to an end as his successor, William I, a Norman, came to the throne.

Studying the Anglo-Saxons gives an opportunity for children to develop their historical skills, such as making inferences from evidence and assessing the reliability of a source, and to appreciate the role of the archaeologist in providing information about the past. There are opportunities for cross-curricular work, particularly in literacy, mathematics and design and technology. In this activity section there are suggestions to support children's work in ICT.

SUGGESTED FURTHER ACTIVITIES

Pages 4 – 5 People on the move
Some of the information we have about the Anglo-Saxons comes from written accounts of people living in England at the time. The children may think that any event would be written about accurately by all the writers. They can explore this idea in the following way, working in pairs. They should walk around the school or outside and then write a short account about it. Let them compare accounts and see where they are similar and different. They could then watch a programme or news item about people moving homes, perhaps as refugees, and write accounts and compare them. From this they could assess the reliability of using just one source that describes an event.

Pages 6 – 7 Who were the Anglo-Saxons?
You may like to plan some role play for which the children dress up in costumes of the time. The following website provides pictures which you can use as a guide for making a costume, perhaps by adapting old clothes. The site also has instructions for making a simple costume. http://www.users.iafrica.com/m/me/melisant/costume/saxon.htm

Pages 8 – 9 The end of Roman Britain
The Romans had forts to act as sea defences against raiding tribes. These were at Brancaster, Caister on Sea, Carisbrook, Porchester, Lymme, Dover, Reculver and Richborough. Let the children use an atlas to find their positions on the coast. Use the map on page 19 to see which of the Anglo-Saxon peoples swept past the different forts.

Pages 10 – 11 The Anglo-Saxons arrive
Having established that one written account of an event may be unreliable (see the activity for pages 4-5), the children can assess the reliability of the Anglo-Saxon Chronicles. Writing a chronicle requires some form of selection by the writer. The children can realise this by keeping a diary for a week in which they write down items from the children's TV news which they find interesting. When they compare their 'chronicles' they can assess the value of using the Anglo-Saxon Chronicles for a complete picture of events in England at the time.

Pages 12 – 13 Sutton Hoo
The children can look at the following two websites and click on the hot spots to find out about the discoveries. First they should try http://www.nationaltrust.org.uk/places/suttonhoo. This allows them to use the mouse to make a panoramic view of the site. Then they should try http://www.suttonhoo.org/ for more detail about the mounds.

Pages 14 – 15 Why was the ship buried?
Some archaeologists perform experiments to help them understand the past. The children could be asked how they think the Anglo-Saxons got the ship to the site. Look for answers about pushing it along or putting it on a wagon. Rule out the wagon as not being strong enough to support the ship and steer the children towards considering the use of rollers. Present them with a large toy ship, pencils (for rollers), a force meter (spring balance) and some sticky paper and ask them to compare the force of dragging the ship and using rollers; then let them suggest which method might have been used to move the Sutton Hoo ship.

Pages 16 – 17 A look at the treasures

The children can look at the treasures and collect pictures for their work from http://www.thebritishmusuem.ac.uk. They should click on Children's compass>tours>Anglo-Saxon England, then the arrow on the right, then the helmet. Ask the children to write down three things that each artefact tells them about the Anglo-Saxons.

Pages 18 – 19 Where the Anglo-Saxons came from

Different groups of Anglo-Saxons put different designs on their cremation pots. This fact has been used to trace the movement of Anglo-Saxons from Europe to England. For example, pots with a design used by some Saxons in Europe have also been found in Norfolk and this suggests that people moved from one area to the other. The children can learn about this by drawing the outlines of six pots using the photograph on page 7 to help them, and drawing a distinctive design on each pair. One pot from each pair is placed in a dish of sand and the dishes are placed at places around the room (representing other countries). The other pots are placed in different positions on a table (representing finds made in different places in the same country). A friend then digs up the pots and matches them with those on the table and the path of the imaginary pot-making people can be traced across the room between the 'countries'.

Pages 20 – 21 Anglo-Saxon settlements

The children can look at pictures of an Anglo-Saxon village at http://www.geocities.com/Athens/2471/westow.html.
They could use the pictures to help them construct a model Anglo-Saxon house, selecting suitable materials for the wooden walls and thatch roof. At the site of some Anglo-Saxon settlements hollows have been found at the foundations of the houses. Some archaeologists believe that the house had a pit beneath it, covered with planks, which served for insulation and kept the floor dry. The children could make a shallow rectangular pit in a tray of damp sand and cover it with planks of card or thin strips of wood (lolly sticks perhaps) to make a foundation for their model house. When the house is in place they can reflect on how the materials of the house rotted away but the pit was left behind.

Pages 22 – 23 Anglo-Saxon farmers

The children can look at a working Anglo-Saxon farm at http://www.bedesworld.co.uk/bedesworld.php, then click on Gyrwe Anglo-Saxon demonstration farm, then on animals and plants. If they visit this site at different times of year and click on 'What's happening', they can learn how the activities on the farm change with the seasons.

Pages 24 – 25 Anglo-Saxon crafts

If the children log onto www.regia.org/village.htm they can visit the village of Wichamstow. You may find the site a little text dense for this age group but they can click on the various craftspeople and look at the colour pictures and read the captions to get an idea of what life was like and how items were made.

Pages 26 – 27 So who was buried in the ship?

You may like the children to review their knowledge of Anglo-Saxon life and the Sutton Hoo artefacts and make a drawing (or a portrait) of how they think the king in the Sutton Hoo grave looked. They could then check their idea with that of an artist who has also constructed a picture of the king at www.gettysburg.edu/academics/english/britain/anglo-saxon/Sutton_Hoo_work_here/identity.html.

ADDITIONAL RESOURCES

Websites

http://www.britainexpress.com/History/anglo-saxon_life.htm
(a straightforward resource covering a large number of aspects of Anglo-Saxon life which is suitable for extra reading by older children).

http://www.britainexpress.com/History/Anglo-Saxon_Britain.htm
(follows from the site above and shows the major kingdoms in early Anglo-Saxon times. It also provides an introduction to Anglo-Saxon kings through a brief study of King Offa).

http://www.britannia.com/history/monarchs/mon21.html
(suitable for more able children – and adults – wishing to find out about all the Anglo-Saxon kings).

http://www.escombsaxonchurch.com/
(shows a Saxon church. Click the history button on the home page for description of the main features, photographs and a church 'tour').

http://www.lothene.org/others/weststow.html
(has plenty of photographs of a reconstruction built up by experimental archaeology. The children may look at this website to get ideas of what life might have been like in an Anglo-Saxon settlement).

Books

The Anglo-Saxon Chronicles translated and collated by Anne Savage (ISBN 0 333 37041 4) is a highly illustrated and attractively presented book suitable for more able children and adults.

Curriculum Bank History 1, Scholastic (ISBN 0 590 53397-5) has a section of lesson plans on Anglo-Saxons with differentiation, assessment activities and photocopiable worksheets.

Anglo-Saxon raiders and settlers is the title of the student book and teacher's guide published by Atlantic Europe Co Ltd which are supported by a picture poster pack and integrated website. They are available at http://www.CurriculumVisions.com.

The Young Archaeologists' Club

The magazine of the Young Archaeologists' Club has up-to-date information on archaeological digs, competitions and quizzes. YAC members can take part in archaeological activities at branches around the country. Contact: The Young Archaeologists' Club, Bowes Morrell House, 111 Walmgate, York YO1 9WA. Telephone 01904 671417. Email: yac@britarch.ac.uk   Website: www.britarch.ac.uk/yac

Index